Zak the Storyteller

Written by Sufiya Ahmed
Illustrated by Adriana Predoi

OXFORD
UNIVERSITY PRESS

Words to look out for ...

benefit VERB
You benefit from something, or it benefits you, when it helps you.

hint NOUN
a slight indication or suggestion

monitor VERB
To monitor something is to watch it or test it regularly, in order to see what is happening.

organize VERB
To organize people is to get them together to do something.

routine NOUN
a regular or fixed way of doing things

sense VERB
To sense something is to feel it or be aware of it.

Chapter 1

Zakir looked out at the quiet street. Except for a ginger cat curled up asleep, there was no one about. Another day had come to an end. The neighbours were all inside their homes.

Zakir wondered if any of *them* had a guest staying with them, too.

"I wish my mummy was here," said a little voice from behind him.

Zakir closed the curtains and turned to face his younger cousin.

Aisha was sitting on the sofa looking sad. She hugged her arms across her chest.

Zakir felt sorry for her.

Aisha's mummy was Zakir's Aunty Shazia. She had a new job where she had to travel to other countries.

For the first time ever, Aisha had come to stay at Zakir's house.

Zakir and his parents loved having Aisha to stay. However, Aisha was not happy. She missed her mum.

"Your mummy will be back in a few days," said Zakir, glancing at the bookshelf.

Perhaps he should read Aisha a story to make her feel better.

Aisha <u>sensed</u> that Zakir was going to suggest a book. She grabbed the blanket on the sofa and pulled it over her head.

To <u>sense</u> something is to feel it or be aware of it.

"I don't want to hear a story," said Aisha in a quiet voice.

Staring at the lump under the blanket, Zakir had an idea.

Perhaps he could make up a story about Aunty Shazia's job. It could be about her doing very important work that would make Aisha proud.

Excitedly, Zakir ran to a cupboard and pulled out a white sheet. Back in the living room, he carefully put the sheet over a chair.

He stepped back and admired his work. He had created an Arctic landscape.

Aisha's head came out from the blanket.

"What are you doing?" she said.

"I'm creating a theatre scene. It will be for my story about your mummy's job. She is saving the planet!"

"You don't know what my mummy is doing!" Aisha said.

"I know all the stories," said Zakir.

"Your mummy is in the Arctic. She is monitoring the ice so the polar bears can be saved," said Zakir. "A bear and her cubs will benefit from her hard work."

At this, Aisha pressed her hands to her ears. "I don't want to hear it!" she yelled.

To monitor something is to watch it or test it regularly, in order to see what is happening.

You benefit from something, or it benefits you, when it helps you.

Zakir's mum walked in. "What's going on in here?" she said.

"Zakir-bhai is saying Mummy is with the polar bears," said Aisha. "They would only eat her."

"Don't scare Aisha," said Mum.

Zakir's shoulders slumped.
He wasn't trying to scare Aisha.
He was only trying to tell a story.

Chapter 2

The next day, Zakir spoke to Dad about his story. He had only wanted to make Aisha happy.

"I see," said Dad. "It was nice of you to do that. Can I help?"

"I'd like to build the pyramids next. I'd need cardboard boxes," said Zakir.

"We could ask the supermarket for some boxes," suggested Dad.

After dinner, Dad helped Zakir build two small pyramids. First, they cut the cardboard into three pieces. Next, they glued them together before putting them on a light brown sheet.

Zakir put on his blue thobe. Aunty Shazia had bought it for him in Egypt.

"Aisha!" he called.

Aisha entered the living room. "What are those triangles?" she said.

Zakir patted the sheet. "Come and sit on the sand. I will tell you about the ancient Egyptians," he said. "There has been a discovery in the desert."

"Some treasure has been dug up. It's been buried for thousands of years! Your mummy is here to monitor the digging. It's important she writes everything down."

"Stop saying that about my mummy!" cried Aisha.

"Don't you want to listen to my story?" said Zakir calmly.

To monitor something is to watch it or test it regularly, in order to see what is happening.

"No!" protested Aisha. "I don't want to hear it! My mummy having to do all that digging and …" She stomped her foot on the sheet, crumpling it.

Mum appeared. "What have you said now, Zakir?" she asked.

Dad was just as surprised as Zakir.

"Nothing!" said Dad.

Mum apologized the next day.

"I'm sorry I snapped at you, Zakir. Dad explained everything. Remember, Aisha is only five. She doesn't understand that you're trying to cheer her up."

"We will keep Aisha happy with a forest today," said Dad.

After school, Zakir gathered lots of pot plants. He put them all into one room.

When Zakir was ready, Dad led Aisha in.

"Enter the rainforest," said Zakir, holding his arms out wide. "Your mummy is looking after the trees."

"Why?" asked a curious Aisha.

"She is organizing a group to stop trees being chopped down. This will benefit the whole planet."

Aisha had opened her mouth to say something but changed her mind.

Dad had clearly talked to Aisha about giving the story a chance.

To organize people is to get them together to do something.

You benefit from something, or it benefits you, when it helps you.

Zakir was about to continue, when Aisha turned to Dad and …

Her elbow hit into a plant pot. The pot smashed on the floor, breaking into pieces.

Aisha stared at the mess. "I didn't mean to do that!" she said.

"It was just an accident," Dad said kindly. "Go and find your aunty. Zakir and I will clean up," he said. He patted her lightly on the head.

Zakir frowned as he bent to sweep up the pieces. So much for his rainforest.

Chapter 3

The next day was Saturday. Aisha and Mum went shopping to prepare for a special dinner. Aunty Shazia was coming home!

Zakir and Dad had their Saturday routine of jobs to do. As Zakir polished the table, he had made up his mind. He was not going to tell any more stories.

A routine is a regular or fixed way of doing things.

"What story are you going to tell today?" asked Dad.

"I'm not going to bother," said Zakir. "Aisha doesn't enjoy them."

"Mum will have a word with Aisha," said Dad. "I'm sure she'll be interested in hearing one today."

Later that day, Aisha walked into the living room. Her eyes instantly grew round with wonder.

Zakir was standing against a black sheet dotted with stars. He was holding a spaceship made from a water bottle.

Aisha smiled. "Aunty said you'd have a story for me," she said.

"Welcome to space!" announced Zakir. "Your mummy is about to take off in this rocket. Let's do the countdown! Ready?"

Zakir began to count down from ten. Aisha joined in with a big voice. "Three, two, one … blast off!" they both shouted.

Zakir lifted the spaceship into the air.

"Aunty Shazia is travelling with a talking robot," said Zakir. "She has to monitor a new planet.

"Wow!" Aisha said. "My mummy's gone into space!"

Suddenly the doorbell rang. Aunty Shazia herself stood in the doorway.

"Mummy!" cried Aisha.

To monitor something is to watch it or test it regularly, in order to see what is happening.

"My darling!" said Aunty Shazia, throwing open her arms.

"You're back!" shouted Aisha.

Aunty Shazia looked around. "What's all this?" she asked.

"Zakir-bhai was telling me about your space trip," said Aisha.

Aunty Shazia needed a hint.

"You've just come back from the spaceship, haven't you?" prompted Zakir.

A hint is a slight indication or suggestion.

"Oh yes, of course," Aunty Shazia said, playing along with Zakir's story. "I chose the perfect gift for our storyteller at the space station, too."

Zakir watched Aunty Shazia take out a beautiful notebook from her bag.

"This is for you," she said. "You can write all your stories down in it."

Zakir hugged the gift tightly to his chest.

"It looks cool," he said. "Thank you, Aunty Shazia."

"You can write about the time when Mummy saved the polar bears," said Aisha. "And about the rainforest," she added.

"Goodness me!" said Aisha's mum. "It sounds like I've been busy!"

"Have you got anything for me?" asked Aisha.

"You can open your present at home," said Aunty Shazia. "Now, did you miss me?"

Aisha shrugged. "Maybe a little."

Zakir and his parents exchanged a look.

"Will you be happy to stay here again when I work?" said Aunty Shazia.

Aisha thought about it for a few seconds.

"Only if Zakir-bhai agrees to tell me more stories," she said.

Everybody laughed.

"Mummy, tell me the story about you and the treasure," said Aisha.

Aunty Shazia's mouth fell open.

"Zakir's story about ancient Egypt," said Dad.

"That was an exciting trip," smiled Aunty Shazia. "Perhaps Zakir can tell you that story instead."

"Maybe later," said Zakir.

He wrote his name in his new book.

Zakir couldn't wait to write down the stories twirling around in his imagination. His head was full of adventures all around the world … and in outer space.